Arise and Call Her Blessed

Arise and Call Her Blessed

*The Seven Words and Seven Scenes
from the Life of Mary*

Mary L. Hickey

Paulist Press
New York/Mahwah, N.J.

Cover design by Brianne Wright

Copyright © 1999 by Mary L. Hickey

All rights reserved. No part of this book may be reproduced or transmitted in any form or by any means, electronic or mechanical, including photocopying, recording, or by any information storage and retrieval system without permission in writing from the Publisher.

Unless noted otherwise, all scripture quotations are taken from the *Holy Bible, New International Version*. Copyright © 1973, 1978, 1984 International Bible Society. Used by permission of Zondervan Bible Publishers.

Library of Congress Cataloging-in-Publication Data

Hickey, Mary L., 1955 –
  Arise and call her blessed : seven words and seven scenes from the life of Mary / Mary L. Hickey.
     p. cm.
  ISBN 0-8091-3883-2
  1. Mary, Blessed Virgin, Saint Meditations. 2. Bible. N.T. Meditations. I. Title.
  BT608.5.H353   1999
  232.91–dc21   99-23024
                                                CIP

Published by Paulist Press
997 Macarthur Boulevard
Mahwah, New Jersey 07430

www.paulistpress.com

Printed and bound in the
United States of America

Contents

Introduction ix

The Seven Words

Word 1	Prudence (Luke 1:34)	3
Word 2	Obedience (Luke 1:38)	8
Word 3	Humility (Luke 1:46-49)	13
Word 4	Witness (Luke 1:50-55)	18
Word 5	Responsibility (Luke 2:48)	23
Word 6	Charity (John 2:3)	28
Word 7	Counsel (John 2:5)	32

The Seven Scenes

Scene 1	Joseph Takes Mary to Live with Him (Matthew 1:18-25)	39
Scene 2	The Flight into Egypt (Matthew 2:13-15)	44
Scene 3	Mary Presents Her Son to God (Luke 2:21-24, 33-35)	49
Scene 4	Mary Follows Jesus on His Divine Mission (Luke 8:19-21)	54
Scene 5	Mary Shares with Jesus in His Darkest Hour (John 19:25-27)	59
Scene 6	Mary Prays with the Apostles for the Coming of the Paraclete (Acts of the Apostles 1:12-14)	63
Scene 7	Mary Takes Her Place in Heaven (Revelation 12:1-6)	68

Conclusion 73

Dedication

To Mary, Mother of God, and to all those who love her

Acknowledgments

First of all, I would like to thank my husband Bob and my children John and Alice for their patience in living with someone who is writing, and their graciousness in letting me have exclusive use of our only computer when I needed it to work on the manuscript for this book.

Thanks also to Fr. Lawrence Boadt and Donna Crilly, my editors at Paulist Press, for the help they have given me in making this book the best our combined efforts could produce, to the honor of God and of Mary, our Blessed Mother.

I would also like to thank Melissa Morgan, Karen Duffy, and the Pataskala Christian Writers' Group for their constant encouragement, friendship, and support. Others who have encouraged me to write include, but are not limited to, the two Bill Lawrences and others at the County Press Newspapers in Newtown Square, Pennsylvania, Theresa Hayes, and Marlene Bagnull and the Greater Philadelphia Christian Writers' Fellowship. Kudos also to Marianne Engelmann, Silvia Zaborowski, Jeanne Osborne, Tracy Boehmer, Robin Krempel, Glenda Reynolds, and all the other great folks at Our Lady of Mt. Carmel Parish in Buckeye Lake, Ohio.

Introduction

Mary is the most revered woman in the world. More statues, paintings, literature, and music have been created to honor Mary, the mother of Jesus, than any other woman in history. The purpose of this book is to help us get to know Mary better through her words as recorded in scripture, in the Gospels of Luke and John. The book's title, *Arise and Call Her Blessed*, is taken from Proverbs 31:28 (NIV). In some sense, the "wife of noble character" described in Proverbs 31 prefigures Mary, although the wife in Proverbs 31 is clearly from a more affluent background.

The Bible readings in the first part of this book consist of all the words of Mary, the mother of Jesus, that are recorded in scripture. Mary's song of praise (the Magnificat) is divided into two sections for study because of its longer length, and also because it contains two distinct themes that are more easily studied separately. The readings in the second part of the book depict seven additional scenes in which Mary figures prominently, but in which the biblical writers did not record any words she spoke.

The Bible thus provides us with seven words and seven actions of Mary for our study and meditation. In biblical times, the number seven symbolized perfection, completeness, or wholeness. We see this in the Old Testament in references to the seven eyes of God (Zec 3:9; 4:2,10) and the seven pillars in the house of Wisdom (Prv 9:1). In Matthew 18:21-22, Jesus emphasizes the critical importance of forgiveness by telling us to forgive not merely seven times, but seventy-seven!

It is best if the Related Bible References in each section of this book are looked up and read immediately after reading Mary's words or the descriptions of her actions. However, if your time is limited, the paragraphs concerning the Bible references can be read instead, and the Bible passages themselves can be looked up and studied when time permits.

The first two Questions in each chapter concern the Bible story itself. In most cases, the questions ask you to explore the feelings, motivations, and intentions that Mary expresses through her words. The Reflections express my own views regarding the passages and their relation to my experiences and perceptions. Feel free to question or disagree with these views. And especially, feel free to add your own ideas.

The second set of Questions in each section do not have "right" or "wrong" answers. Their purpose is to help you relate your own life to Mary's, and to relate the problems she faced to the issues we encounter today. They are invitations to gain a deeper understanding of the mind and heart of Mary, the mother of Jesus. I hope that the resulting empathy with Mary will lead us to a better appreciation and understanding of ourselves and one another, and finally of how God himself works in our lives.

THE SEVEN WORDS

Word 1

Prudence (Luke 1:34)

"How will this be," Mary asked the angel, "since I am a virgin?"

Main Bible Story

Begin by reading the above quote in context, in Luke 1:26-34. Stop at this point. We will cover the angel's answer to this question, and Mary's response, in Word 2.

Related Bible References

To understand this passage fully, it helps to compare Mary's response to the angel to Zechariah's in Luke 1:8-25. Zechariah, too, has received a visit from an angel informing him that he will soon be the parent of a son. In verse 18, Zechariah says, "How can I be sure of this? I am an old man and my wife is well along in years." The wording is different in subtle ways that show the very different dispositions of these two people who received similar messages from angels.

This difference in wording is not just the result of differing translations of the Bible. For example, the King James Version has Mary saying, "How shall this be...?" and Zechariah saying, "Whereby shall I know this...?" No matter which translation is used, it appears that Mary is asking a simple question for the purpose of clarification, but Zechariah is demanding a sign because of his unbelief. The angel's response (cordial to Mary, angry with Zechariah) in each case suggests that these interpretations are indeed correct.

Mary asks for more information only for her peace of mind. Her heart has already consented to obey the Lord. Zechariah asks for a sign, then, because his heart is rebellious, uses his mind to come up with obstacles and to challenge the word of God.

Questions Regarding the Bible Story

1. How does Mary's question to the angel differ from Zechariah's response? Are the words important, or the attitude?

2. Why was Mary " greatly troubled" by the angel's message? Do you think she was anxious or worried, or simply overwhelmed by the importance of the commission she had just received?

Reflection

Prudence is using our minds as well as our hearts in our efforts to serve God as best we are able. It means thinking and planning ahead, while still allowing God to be in charge. In Mary's case, it meant asking a key question to be sure that she understood what God intended her to do.

Another example of questioning in a spirit of obedience, as Mary did, is Jesus' prayer in the garden of Gethsemane (see Mt 26:36-46) where he asks that if possible, this "cup" be taken away from him. Jesus isn't indecisive about his obedience to the Father. However, he does want to be certain that the terrible suffering and death looming before him are in fact necessary. It would be rather pessimistic for us always to assume that the most difficult and painful of the choices before us are what God wants! There is no sin in avoiding needless suffering. Sin enters in if we are unwilling to take the road the Lord requires, which of course may mean hardship and suffering.

If we are too fearful of God to ask any questions, or to use our own minds to plan the best way to carry out his commands for fear of making a mistake and incurring his wrath, we underestimate his love for us. Perhaps we are comparing God to people who have authority over us on Earth. A subordinate can have an open and trusting relationship with someone who holds power over him or her only in an atmosphere of unconditional love, which cannot fully exist in any human power relationship. But our bad experiences with bosses, teachers, and perhaps even parents must not set the pattern for our relationship with God.

The virtue of prudence causes us to carry out the Lord's commands in the best way possible, in accord with our abilities and limitations. It may mean delaying action until the best possible moment, rather than impetuously rushing in and succeeding only in making a bad impression. Prudence is not to be confused with procrastination, which is delaying out of fear or unwillingness in an attempt to avoid doing what God asks of us. True prudence complements obedience to God by bringing our human resources, as best we can, into conformity with his will.

Questions Relating the Story to Our Lives and Times

1. When should you question what the Lord asks of you? Do some things "feel wrong" even as you pray about them? If they do, it may be a warning that either something is wrong or you do not yet understand what God wants in the situation you are facing. That is when you need to pray for insight and the strength to accept his final decision.

2. Do you pray before making major decisions? How do you know when the Lord is giving you an answer? What do you do if the answer is not what you had hoped for? Again, there is nothing wrong with praying for help in accepting what God has

decided if our mental and spiritual resources don't seem to be "up to it."

3. How does a question asked in faith differ from one asked with unreasonable doubt and perhaps pride? Ask God to help you understand what he is doing if it isn't obvious to you. He knows our limitations and wants to help us get past them, if only we will ask!

4. Can a refusal to ask any questions of God sometimes be due to fear rather than faith? Are you ever afraid that what God will ask will be so awful that you'd rather not know about it? Thinking of God's incomprehensible love for us can help us overcome this fear. Then we can ask our questions in faith, with a heart that is willing to listen and follow our Lord.

Word 2

Obedience (Luke 1:38)

"I am the Lord's servant," Mary answered. "May it be to me as you have said."

Main Bible Story

Start by reading the above quote in context, beginning where you left off in Word 1, Luke 1:35-38.

Related Bible References

The familiar Bible story of Noah building the ark, which begins at Genesis 6:5, shows the great lengths to which a believer will go to carry out a command he is sure is the word of God. Noah surely suffered ridicule as well as callused hands and sore muscles as he labored to build the ark that would save him and his family from the flood. The ark itself was surely crowded, noisy, and smelly. Yet, having come that far, Noah could rest assured that the Lord would in the end restore his fortunes and reward him for his faithfulness. We see that happen in Genesis 9.

The story of Abraham sacrificing Isaac (Gn 22:1-18) is another example of trusting obedience. Abraham did not obey out of fear, but rather he believed that somehow everything would turn out well, as he shows in his response to his son's question about where they will get a sheep to sacrifice (Gn 22:8).

Both of these stories are examples of trust and obedience, but also of God's will being accomplished with human cooperation. Passivity before God is not enough. It would seem logical to think that God, being infinite and eternal, would have no need or use for people who are relatively powerless and doomed to die. Yet over and over, we find that what people do matters a lot to their Creator.

Questions Regarding the Bible Story

1. Why doesn't Mary need to ask for more time to consider the angel's request?

2. Why didn't Mary feel any need to consult Joseph about this request?

Reflection

Obedience is doing the will of another, at the other's request or command, rather than acting on one's own will. Obedience can be willing and trustful, as, for example, when the various biblical patriarchs heard God speak to them and did as he asked. Abraham was even willing to sacrifice his only son, Isaac, when the Lord asked it of him (Gn 22:1-18). But obedience can also be a heavy burden, filled with fear, loathing, and distrust, as it was for the Israelites when they obeyed the Egyptians while they were slaves in that country.

Mary's acquiescence to the will of God was willing, not fearful. Fear is a natural emotion in the face of absolute power, and the Bible's authors, inspired by the Holy Spirit, went to great pains to calm the fears of God's people. Obedience has dignity when it is given to someone worthy of it—that is, to God or to those acting by God's authority—such as the obedience children owe to their parents. Obedience is only demeaning when it is given to someone or something that is unworthy of it, such as a violent, repressive, and atheistic government, or our own carnal desires that quickly get out of hand if indulged in ways God has forbidden.

Obedience is a difficult concept for a twentieth-century American, brought up to value freedom and liberty and to fight to the death for these values, as our ancestors did in the Revolution. The platitude that obedience actually leads to greater freedom seems contradictory and illogical. But obedience to God is not like obedience to a human authority that is using us for his or her own purposes, which may or may not be worthy. To obey God willingly, we must first understand as best that we can the depth of his knowledge of us and his love for us. Then we will understand that what he asks of us will work out better and make us happier in the end than following our own impulses would have.

Obedience can begin with a less than perfect attitude. Jonah started out as an unwilling prophet. He only submitted to the will of God after it became evident that he could not escape it. He would have been content to remain ordinary and be soon forgotten after his death. But God had greater, not lesser, things in mind for Jonah to achieve through obedience to him. Despite Jonah's initial efforts to avoid greatness, God had mercy on his weakness, spared his life, and gave him his place among the prophets. In the end, God uses the incident with the gourd vine (Jon 4:5-11) to help Jonah understand God's love for all people, and to see why what Jonah had done was so important.

Questions Relating the Story to Our Lives and Times

1. Why does God choose to depend on us to accomplish his will in the world? In our families? In our culture? Throughout the Bible, God refers to himself as the father (and sometimes the mother—see Luke 13:34, where Jesus compares God to a mother hen who longs to gather her chicks under her protective wings) of the people he has created. Like any parent, he wants to involve his children in what he is doing, to whatever extent they are capable based on their abilities and maturity.

2. When people disobey God, what happens? How can it be alleviated? (See Jonah 3:1-10 to see how quickly God forgives when people who had provoked his anger repent, and what those people do as an outward sign of their inward change of heart. In Joel 2:11-27, we can see that God promises forgiveness and restoration even if he has already begun punishing his people because they are doing evil and have so far not repented of it.)

3. How can we cooperate with the will of God? How do we discover what it is, without an angel appearing to tell us? The

power of prayer is greater than anyone on Earth imagines, and God's word is an indispensable guide. Do you have a Bible handy at home? If you don't, why not go out and buy one today?

Word 3

Humility (Luke 1:46-49)

And Mary said:

46 *"My soul glorifies the Lord*
47 *and my spirit rejoices in God my savior,*
48 *for he has been mindful*
of the humble state of his servant.
From now on all generations will call me blessed,
49 *for the Mighty One has done great things for me—*
holy is his name."

Main Bible Story

Word 3 introduces the first part of the Magnificat, Mary's song of praise for the blessing she has received from God in accord with the message of the angel. The Magnificat is one of the most beloved of all Bible passages. At the Shrine of the Visitation at Ain Karem, believed to be the town where Mary visited Elizabeth, there is a wall displaying Mary's song of praise in over one hundred languages. The story of the Visitation is recounted in the continuation of Luke 1, verses 39-49.

Related Bible References

Breaking forth into a spontaneous song of joy and thanksgiving when the Lord has granted a signal favor seems to have been a common response in biblical times. Among the women of the Bible, three others stand out for responding this way to a blessing: Deborah (Jgs 5:2-31), Hannah (1 Sm 2:1-10), and Miriam (Ex 15:20-21), for whom Mary was probably named. Deborah praises the Lord for the decisive defeat of Israel's enemies, which leads into a forty-year period of peace, and Miriam leads the Israelite women in praise for the parting of the Red Sea and the destruction of Pharaoh's army. But the song of Hannah is the one that most resembles Mary's Magnificat, and it was composed in response to a similar favor, the gift of a son.

All these women praised what God had done for them without false modesty. Sometimes it is hard to do this without it sounding like bragging. Mary avoids this by noting her own humble state, that all the power came from God, not something she did to deserve it—she had never asked to be the mother of the coming Messiah, nor tried to do anything to earn the privilege. She also points out that the blessing God has given her is for everyone, including future generations, not just for her. But since the blessing was given through her, she predicts that others will preserve her memory and describe her as "blessed."

Questions Regarding the Bible Story

1. Did Mary spend time working on the Magnificat? Did she have to labor over it?
2. Why did Mary choose to share her joy first with Elizabeth?

Reflection

Humility is the knowledge and acceptance of one's own humble and flawed nature. Humility flows naturally from awestruck awareness of the greatness, wisdom, and love of God, and of our own insignificance before his majesty.

Mary's prophetic canticle flowed spontaneously from her heart as naturally as a river flows from its source to the sea in the path God has ordained for it. It was the product of a humble heart overwhelmed by the greatness of what God would accomplish through her. She did not embellish the facts, since they were amazing enough in themselves. She simply shared the great news that had been given to her with the person most likely to understand, the kinswoman mentioned by the angel Gabriel in his conversation with her.

Mary understood that she was not personally capable of carrying out what God had asked of her. She would need to be "blessed" by God, that is, inspired and empowered, to be the human mother of his son. This knowledge of her own inadequacy does not lead her to become discouraged or depressed. Instead, she is confident God will in fact bless her, fulfilling his promise as she carries out what she has told the angel she would do. We can share in this confidence as long as we are carrying out the will of God, not just our own plans that may or may not be pleasing to him.

Questions Relating the Story to Our Lives and Times

1. How does sharing a blessing, as Mary did with Elizabeth, help our walk in the Lord? How do we know with whom to share what God has done for us? If our family is unreceptive, where can we go to share our blessings with others?

2. Mary knew that for centuries there had been prophecies regarding the coming of the Messiah. These prophecies indicated that the event would be public and visible, and not a private and hidden event. How do we know when a blessing we receive from God is, like the angelic message Mary received, bread to be shared with others, or when it is more like a medicine formulated just for us?

3. Do unbelievers sometimes seem to resent your witness about what God has done for you, thinking you are bragging that you are on the fast track? How can you set them at ease and reassure them that God will do the same for them if they turn their hearts to him?

Word 4

Witness (Luke 1:50-55)

*50 His mercy extends to those who fear him,
    from generation to generation.
51 He has performed mighty deeds with his arm;
    he has scattered those who are proud in their
    inmost thoughts.
52 He has brought down rulers from their thrones
    and has lifted up the humble.
53 He has filled the hungry with good things
    but has sent the rich away empty.
54 He has helped his servant Israel,
    remembering to be merciful
55 to Abraham and his descendants forever,
    even as he said to our fathers.*

Main Bible Story

This passage is the continuation and completion of the Magnificat, Mary's song of praise. After this, Mary disappears from the scene in verse 56, which tells us she stayed with Elizabeth for about three months and then returned home. Since the angel had told her that "she who was said to be barren is in her sixth month" (Lk 1:36), Mary no doubt assisted with the birth of John the Baptist, then returned to her own home, where she would have had her baby had not the census decree intervened (Lk 2:1-7).

Related Bible References

In Word 1, it was helpful to compare Mary's response to the angel to Zechariah's. Here, it also helps to compare Mary's canticle with that of Zechariah, after his dumbness is healed, in Luke 1:68-79. Though Zechariah started out in disbelief almost to the point of mockery, when his doubts were allayed, he understood the plan of God in much the same way that Mary did.

Mary and Zechariah both fully understood that the seemingly humble and simple events in which they were taking part had implications for all time and for all peoples and places, but in a special way for God's chosen people. When Jesus was born, Simeon, in his song of praise, brought the extension of God's mercy to all people, Jew and Gentile alike, into clearer focus. In Luke 2:29-32, Simeon joyfully proclaims to God that he may "now dismiss your servant in peace" because he has seen the promised Messiah, who will be "a light for revelation to the Gentiles and for glory to your people Israel" (Lk 2:32).

As noted in Word 3, Mary's Magnificat can be compared to Hannah's prayer of praise in 1 Samuel 2:1-10. Both make special mention of the Lord's dominion over wealth and poverty, victory and defeat in war, and the relative position in society of both the humble and the proud. Mary speaks here of a God of both justice and mercy, who will overthrow the entire social order if necessary to bring about his kingdom on Earth.

Questions Regarding the Bible Story

1. To what historical events might Mary be referring in verses 51 and 52?
2. What biblical examples can you recall of God's mercy to the people of Israel?

Reflection

Witness is sharing the gift of God with others. When we witness for God, we help carry out Jesus' "Great Commission" to spread the gospel throughout the world. We can start with our own families, friends, neighbors, and coworkers.

Mary begins her Magnificat with a personal hymn of praise, recognizing and overflowing with gratitude for what the Lord has done for her. Only then does she attempt to extend the blessing to other generations (Lk 1:48), to the humble and hungry (Lk 1:52-53), and finally to "Abraham and his descendants," that is, all whom God has called (Lk 1:54-55). What we do not have, or do not recognize that we have, or do not accept as God's gift to us, we cannot share with others or put to use in the Lord's service, as the two good servants did in the parable of the talents (Mt 25:14-30). This shows the importance for all of us of prayers of praise, so that we fully recognize our giftedness and do not lapse into inactivity because of false humility, fear, discouragement over setbacks, or depression.

The women's songs of praise recorded in the Bible would never have been remembered by anyone if their authors had simply hummed them to themselves as they went to draw water from the wells. These songs were acts of witness and serve as examples of how even a person who holds no authority over anyone else can nonetheless change the world by expressing his or her faith. The power of God's word does not depend on where we stand in human power structures, but comes instead from God himself.

Questions Relating the Story to Our Lives and Times

1. Does submission to God's will unleash creativity for you, as it did for Mary? How can proper submission to God's will be distinguished from a passive indifference that could lead to the unscriptural burying of talents?

2. Have you seen God's hand in some of the most important historical events of our times, as Mary did? How do you know it was God at work? Was what actually happened a factor, or was it the seemingly overwhelming odds against the event, at least when only worldly factors were considered, that demonstrated the work of God?

3. Not everyone who is proud displays it openly. How can we tell if people, perhaps ourselves, are "proud in their inmost thoughts"? What does it mean to be humble?

4. What is the role of Mary's evident joy in God in her witness to Elizabeth? When we witness, do we ever try too hard to make an intellectually convincing case for our faith, but not showcase the fruit of joy that it bears?

Word 5

Responsibility (Luke 2:48)

When his parents saw him, they were astonished. His mother said to him, "Son, why have you treated us like this? Your father and I have been anxiously searching for you."

Main Bible Story

Begin by reading this quotation in context, in Luke 2:21-42. We learn here that loss of a child while traveling happened even to the very best of families the Earth has known. Mary's reaction will no doubt ring true to any mother who has had this frightening experience.

Related Bible References

In Galatians 4:1-2, we read that while he is still a child, the heir is treated no differently than a servant. Jesus is the heir to all that the Father created, yet he lived with Joseph and Mary as a child subject to their authority. His example ennobles this subjection, making it no embarrassment not to be completely free to do as one pleases but instead have various obligations because one bows to a higher authority.

In Ephesians 6:1-3, Paul instructs children to obey their parents, reminding them of the ancient commandment to "honor thy father and mother." Jesus knew this commandment, and was subject to his parents until the time came for him to begin his mission outside his home in Nazareth (see Words 6 and 7, concerning the wedding in Cana). Going to the temple was not an act of disobedience on the boy Jesus' part, as evidenced by Mary's reaction after she got over her initial strong feelings of anxiety and then relief. Luke records that she "treasured all these things in her heart." This seems to imply that the memory was a wonder-filled, beautiful one, not a rueful one, as are many parents' memories of incidents in which their children were temporarily lost.

Questions Regarding the Bible Story

1. Why did Joseph and Mary not miss Jesus right away?
2. Why did Jesus not tell his parents he intended to return to the temple?

Reflection

Responsibility is accepting one's duties as well as one's rights, and carrying out these duties reliably, faithfully, and willingly. Responsibility also means obeying those who rightfully have authority over us. First in line, of course, is God himself. If we have not accepted his kingship over us, it will be very hard to submit to any lesser authority, even when rebellion would be inappropriate and pointless.

Jesus put God first in authority over him. This was the only love, and the only duty, that he put ahead of his love for his parents and his duty to be subject to them. When one has a duty to submit to earthly authority, and to do so does not violate the laws of God, then it is a sign of strength rather than weakness to choose to follow the way the Lord has ordained. Working together with others within an organized structure such as a family, business, or nation can result in less wasted time and effort, and in the end less frustration. One can join in such cooperative works without loss of freedom of heart and mind.

Jesus had to make his decision to obey the Father on his own, despite having the most faith-filled parents any child ever could or will have. There is a limit to how much faith can be "instilled" by even the most well-meaning parents. In the end, every person must make his or her own decision to follow the Lord. Perhaps this is why Mary treasured this memory so dearly. It was evidence that her son had accepted the divine calling that had been revealed to her by the angel when she made her own decision of faith at the time of Jesus' conception.

Questions Relating the Story to Our Lives and Times

1. If a child you know, perhaps your own, were lost, is the church the first place you would look? (Would the possibility even cross your mind?)

2. Mary didn't "keep tabs" on Jesus, making sure he was with them when they left. He had to have known the caravan was packing and would soon leave. She trusted him. What inspires a parent to trust a child? (Not just age, surely. Some children can be trusted at eight, and others can't be trusted at twenty-one!)

3. How do we know when our children are finding the Lord on their own, and when they need a firm push from the adults in their lives? (See Matthew 7:16, where Jesus tells us that with people as with trees, "By their fruit you will recognize them.")

4. Why does the author take care to note that Mary "treasured all these things in her heart"? If you have children, what memories of their early years do you treasure? What events

from your own life, especially your childhood, do you "treasure in your heart"? To whom do you reveal them, and when?

5. When God seems to be missing from your life, do you actively search for him? Is the church one of the places you look?

Word 6

Charity (John 2:3)

When the wine was gone, Jesus' mother said to him, "They have no more wine."

Main Bible Story

Words 6 and 7 tell the story of Jesus' first miracle, the changing of the water into wine at the wedding in Cana. The story begins with John 2:1-3. Stop at this point. We will cover Jesus' response, Mary's further actions, and the eventual outcome, in Word 7.

Related Bible References

In John 2:1-3, Mary is mentioned twice, and both times is referred to as "Jesus' mother." Other biblical women, when mentioned because of something they did, are generally referred to by name. Mary's motherhood was obviously something very special to John. Yet this story recounts the day that

Jesus parts company with his family and begins his long journey that will end with a cross on Calvary.

Mary is not the only person in the New Testament who intercedes with Jesus that he use his power to solve friends' and family members' problems that seem impervious to human solutions alone. Martha and Mary intercede on Lazarus's behalf by simply telling Jesus, "The one you love is sick" (Jn 11:3). Jairus asks Jesus to heal his daughter (Mk 6:21-24, 35-43). The centurion asks for healing for his servant (Lk 7:1-10). Most remarkable of all, the Canaanite woman continues to plead for her daughter despite what appears to be a stinging rebuff (Mk 7:24-30). But in the end she, too, receives what she had asked for.

Questions Regarding the Bible Story

1. Why did the servants ask Mary to try to get Jesus to do something about their problem?

2. Why did Mary turn to Jesus first when the wine ran out, instead of perhaps offering to go out and buy some more wine?

Reflection

Charity is genuine concern for the needs of others, born of love for them. Sometimes we express charity by doing something to help those in need, whether we know them or not, in the manner of the Good Samaritan. Other times we can do nothing ourselves, and so resort to intercessory prayer for others. Intercessory prayer specifically addressed to Jesus had its beginning with Mary's "hint" to him at Cana.

The way that Mary addresses this request to her son shows her recognition that the time for her to have authority over Jesus, the son of God, is at an end. In a way, Jesus is being courteous to her by saying his time has not yet come. Instead of rebelling against the authority of a mother over her son, in a spirit of charity he is making her insist on relinquishing it, which she does. Though letting go of her only son may have been just as hard for her as for any other parent, she shows here that she has managed to make the transition away from an adult-child relationship with her son. In this story, she clearly relates to Jesus as another adult.

Mary was charitable enough to observe the need for more wine before the family giving the wedding was publicly embarrassed by this evidence of their lack of resources, foresight, or generosity. Mary does not pass judgment on why they ran out of wine, and neither does Jesus. In love and charity, they show their concern, she by interceding and he by miraculous intervention to solve the problem at hand. When we intercede in prayer for the needs of others, we do best simply to present the needs to God and leave both the judging and the course of action up to him.

Questions Relating the Story to Our Lives and Times

1. When you see an obvious need, do you pray about it right away? Or do you try to handle it entirely on your own? What finally convinces you to pray about the situation?

2. How can intercessory prayer make you feel less helpless in the face of what appear to be insurmountable problems?

3. What are some opportunities for intercessory prayer during a "normal" day? When we hear an ambulance pass our house, we can pray for whoever is in trouble, even if we have no idea who it might be. We can pray when we pass a school or a government building, that those inside will be given the light they need to do God's work. What other opportunities for prayer can you think of?

4. Do you bring everything to the Lord in prayer, or are there areas of your life you feel are not right to bring to him? For example, do you pray for help if you need to diet or start an exercise program? Why or why not? This story shows that even asking for help with an activity that might be considered "borderline" at best, such as serving a great deal of wine at a social event, is not beyond the pale. God tolerates human enjoyment and recreation more than we often believe.

Word 7

Counsel (John 2:5)

His mother said to the servants,
"Do whatever he tells you."

Main Bible Story

The story of Jesus' first miracle, and his mother's role in it, continues in John 2:4-11.

Related Bible References

Mary already knew that her instruction, "Do whatever he tells you," would be sufficient. She knew from experience that when she herself had done what was asked of her by God, he had taken charge and done all the rest of the work.

The theme of choosing to obey God has recurred throughout this book, and this choice was nothing new to the people of Jesus' time. They were all familiar with the exhortations of Deuteronomy 10 and 11, to "observe the Lord's commands and decrees" (Dt 10:13). They also knew of the promise of reward if they did (Dt 11:13-15) and the threat of a curse if they did not (Dt 11:16-17). Still, they knew they had to make the choice between obedience and disobedience, between the blessing and the curse (Dt 11:26-28).

They also would have known the story of Naaman, who had a hard time believing that washing seven times in the Jordan would cure his leprosy. He was right, of course. You can't just wash away leprosy, in the Jordan or anywhere else. What opened the way for him to be healed was his obedience to God, in his word as given to him through the prophet Elisha (2 Kgs 5). So also at the wedding in Cana, the water was made wine not because the servants filled the water jars, but because they obeyed the Lord.

Questions Regarding the Bible Story

1. How could Mary have been so sure that Jesus could solve the problem? (Was it the events she had "treasured in her heart" that gave her this confidence?)

2. Why did Jesus already have disciples, though he had up to then performed no miracles?

Reflection

Counsel is the ability to advise others in the wisdom of God. In order to advise others, we must first know about the wisdom of God ourselves. One excellent way to acquire this knowledge is to do what you have already been doing by reading this book, that is, learning about God's word from the Bible.

Mary knew Jesus could solve the problem at hand, but since she didn't know exactly how he would do it, she simply advised the waiters to do what he would tell them to do. It isn't always easy to find out what act of faith God is asking of us. Sometimes we need the wise counsel of others to show us where to begin. For us, "filling the water jars" might mean trying to raise believing children in a world that seems to have lost its faith, seeking a job for the first time in years, or learning to do something difficult for us. For one person, it might mean making the first gesture of friendship to a cranky neighbor or to someone who has hurt him or her. For another, it might mean volunteering at the local food pantry or running for the school board.

Mary's instruction, "Do whatever he tells you," was an instruction given and received in a spirit of joy. What Jesus then told them to do was not that difficult to accomplish. The servants had probably filled those same jars hundreds of times. What God asked of them was not completion of the task, but only an act of faith to start it. The Lord will provide the wine for us, too, if we will only fill the water jars.

"Do whatever he tells you." This is the last word the Bible records Mary speaking directly. It is also her last word, her eternal word, to us.

Questions Relating the Story to Our Lives and Times

1. We know that Mary's memories of the miraculous circumstances of Jesus' conception and birth led her to an unwavering faith in him thirty years later. How can we keep alive the memories of answered prayer in our lives? Do you keep some kind of journal to record what God has done for you and your family? Even if you don't write in it regularly, but only now and then, it may prove to be of great help and inspiration to future generations. If your great-grandmother had kept such a journal, wouldn't you read it if you had the chance?

2. The first step for Mary in obtaining Jesus' help was to recognize the need. Can you think of friends or family members who have obvious needs that you have as yet never prayed about?

3. Which of Jesus' instructions from the New Testament do you find most difficult to carry out? Which ones have changed

your life the most as you have carried them out? If we do what God asks of us, he will bless what we do, even when it seems rather insignificant, as it must have to the servants who filled the water jars. He will also bless our efforts when our weakness causes them to be imperfect.

THE SEVEN SCENES

Mary also appears prominently in the Bible in several places where she does not actually speak. In this next part of the book, we explore Mary's role in those incidents and discuss what they mean to us now. Though Mary's words have not been recorded here, she participates in every scene in a meaningful way through her actions and simply by her presence.

This presence alone means a great deal to all of us, and especially to women, because it shows that this woman did participate in every way in the mission of Jesus Christ. When questions arise regarding the propriety of women taking part in some permitted but not necessarily customary aspect of the life of the church Jesus founded, there is often a parallel to one of these scenes or to one of those in the first part of the book. And in either case, the answer may come from Mary, or simply be Mary.

For each of the seven scenes, we include a verse from Proverbs 31 that relates in some way to what Mary was doing at the time. Mary was like the woman described in Proverbs 31: she was active, prayerful, strong, and secure, and lived her life fully and freely despite the constraints of her times. As in the first part of the book, the Reflections express my views regarding the scenes and Mary's part in them. Feel free to extend these ideas by adding your own, and explore aspects that occur to you as you meditate on them.

Scene 1

Joseph Takes Mary to Live with Him (Matthew 1:18-25)

18 This is how the birth of Jesus came about: His mother Mary was pledged to be married to Joseph, but before they came together, she was found to be with child through the Holy Spirit.
19 Because Joseph her husband was a righteous man and did not want to expose her to public disgrace, he had in mind to divorce her quietly.
20 But after he had considered this, an angel of the Lord appeared to him in a dream and said, "Joseph, son of David, do not be afraid to take Mary home as your wife, because what is conceived in her is from the Holy Spirit.
21 She will give birth to a son, and you are to give him the name Jesus, because he will save his people from their sins."
22 All this took place to fulfill what the Lord had said through the prophet:
23 "The virgin will be with child and will give birth to

a son, and they will call him Immanuel"—which means, "God with us."

24 When Joseph woke up, he did what the angel of the Lord had commanded him and took Mary home as his wife.

25 But he had no union with her until she gave birth to a son. And he gave him the name Jesus.

Reference to Proverbs 31

Verse 11: "Her husband has full confidence in her and lacks nothing of value."

Related Bible References

The prophecy quoted by Matthew in verse 23 is from Isaiah 7:14. It is slipped into a Bible chapter that mainly predicts divine punishment for Israel because of its bad conduct and rejection of their God. But in Isaiah, chapter 9, the prophet goes on to speak of redemption and the banishment of the evil that has angered God, which is to come about through the promised Messiah. Among the titles the Messiah will hold are Wonderful Counselor, Mighty God, Everlasting Father, and Prince of Peace (Is 9:6).

No doubt Joseph was familiar with all these prophecies and longed for their fulfillment. He shows his willingness to assume the role to which he has been called by God, just as his wife Mary had already done, by naming the child she bears Jesus, meaning "God with us."

Questions Regarding This Incident in Mary's Life

1. Why did Joseph not believe Mary's explanation of her pregnancy until he heard it from an angel in a dream? Would you have believed it if you were in his place?

2. How did the name of Jesus bring Joseph and Mary together regarding the child she was soon to bear? (See Luke 1:31, where the angel gives Mary the same name for the child as he gives here to Joseph.)

Reflection

Joseph's first reaction to Mary's pregnancy seems to prefigure Jesus' lenient treatment of the woman caught in adultery (Jn 8:1-11), and his respectful manner with the woman at the well who had already had five husbands and was now living with a man to whom she was not married. The law and its enforcers were harsh regarding sexual sin, especially when women committed it, but Jesus always showed compassion to those who sinned through this weakness. Joseph's intentions before he learned the true nature of Mary's pregnancy show that he must have felt similarly, despite this prevailing attitude.

By doing as the angel asked him, Joseph showed he was willing to obey God even in matters that he would have a hard time explaining to his family or neighbors. No doubt Mary was delighted that God had chosen such a principled and considerate man to be her guardian while she carried out his purpose in raising the Messiah to manhood. In the home that she would share with Joseph, she would be able to express herself fully and with complete trust and confidence. She would be a helper to him without being required to bury her own talents in order to be a good wife and mother. They would have the kind of family life God had originally planned for the people created in his image, with the woman as a partner and completer of man, not in any way a mere appendage or piece of property.

Joseph may have understood God's will regarding family life better than his contemporaries in part because the angel Gabriel had first appeared to Mary, not him, at the time of the Annunciation (Lk 1:26–38). And as we noted in The Seven Words, the angel did not require her to seek Joseph's or anyone else's permission to agree to what God asked of her. Joseph will be the leader in their home, as was customary, but it will free Mary, not enslave her; it will reduce stress on her, not increase it. She will have sufficient responsibility and demands on her time and talent in managing the home and raising their divine son to manhood. In a home where all are respected and everyone's gifts are put to use, the family can work and carry its burdens together, and so complete its mission in God.

Questions Relating the Story to Our Lives and Times

1. How does a culture's harsh treatment of unwed pregnancy affect people's perception of the value of human life in general?

2. What are the fruits of this attitude? How does it affect the debate regarding legal abortion?

3. How can a society encourage moral behavior without leaning too heavily on those who sin in this area?

Scene 2

The Flight into Egypt
(Matthew 2:13–15)

13 When they had gone, an angel of the Lord appeared to Joseph in a dream. "Get up," he said, "take the child and his mother and escape to Egypt. Stay there until I tell you, for Herod is going to search for the child to kill him."
14 So he got up, took the child and his mother during the night and left for Egypt,
15 where he stayed until the death of Herod. And so was fulfilled what the Lord had said through the prophet: "Out of Egypt I called my son."

Related Bible References

In verse 15, Matthew refers to Hosea 11:1, where the prophet rebukes Israel for breaking faith with God, who had brought them out of slavery in Egypt. By being sent into exile in Egypt, then returning, the child Jesus reenacts this journey as a redemptive pilgrimage. But instead of breaking faith, Jesus will do what God had originally intended: leave Egypt to live in accord with God's will and covenant in the Promised Land.

Reference to Proverbs 31

Verse 17: "She sets about her work vigorously;
her arms are strong for her tasks."

In Psalm 106, the psalmist recounts the times that Moses and Phinehas interceded with God on behalf of the people shortly after they left Egypt through the Red Sea. The psalm ends with a prayer that God will once again redeem them (Ps 106:47). The writer seems to be praying for another great leader, chosen by God and infused with his spirit, to come and rescue the people once again by interceding with God on their behalf as Moses and Phinehas had done at the time of the Exodus. Jesus' following the road these great leaders had walked provides a parallel with their role in saving the Israelites from the evils that had come upon them because of their disobedience.

Questions Regarding This Incident in Mary's Life

1. What might the Egyptian rulers have done if Herod had discovered Jesus' presence among them and demanded his immediate extradition?

2. Do you think that the Holy Family's Egyptian neighbors ever suspected there was anything different about them?

Reflection

In biblical times, just as in our own, the nation of Israel frequently had problems with its neighbors. Kingdoms and empires came and went in the northern regions, but Egypt was always there in the south. Israel had a special relationship with this country, even though it was often antagonistic. The Israelites had lived in Egypt for many years, even though they had been slaves at the time. And another Joseph had taken refuge there to escape from his own brothers as far back as Genesis, though he, too, had not originally intended to go there (Gn 37:36).

The fact that it was actually safer to keep Israel's infant Messiah in Egypt rather than in his own country prefigures the rejection of Jesus by his own people and his eventual acceptance by many people of other races and nations. Even at the time of his crucifixion, the only person of any authority to acknowledge Jesus as "King of the Jews" publicly will be Pilate, the Roman procurator, over the strident objections of Israel's chief priests (Jn 19:19-22).

Like the Egyptians, we too have a special relationship with the Jewish people. As Catholics, we accept Mary as our mother and Jesus as our brother, making us part of God's family. In some sense we now *are* Jews, spiritually if not ethnically. We have been joined to God's chosen people and share with them the calling that God originally gave only to the Jews—to be the light that draws all the world to him. We have also become co-heirs to the promises God made to Abraham and the other biblical patriarchs.

Mary didn't require another angel's visit for her to be convinced that God had spoken to Joseph. She had already seen and experienced enough of God's care and protection to believe that by entrusting her to Joseph's care, God was ensuring that she would receive whatever she needed. She knew God would arrange for his will to be carried out through her, as she had agreed at the time of the Annunciation. Joseph himself had already demonstrated that he was a godly and compassionate man. He had already heeded the angel's message, given him in a dream, about accepting Mary as his wife and about the name to be given to her child. Unlike Zechariah (Lk 1:8-20), Joseph doesn't look for loopholes.

Questions Relating the Story to Our Lives and Times

1. How can modern Christian couples follow the example of the Holy Family today?

2. How can a family know if it is being called by God to do something special for him?

3. How can we know whether or not something that claims to be a heavenly message, vision, or prophecy is actually from God?

Scene 3

Mary Presents Her Son to God
(Luke 2:21-24, 33-35)

21 On the eighth day, when it was time to circumcise him, he was named Jesus, the name the angel had given him before he had been conceived.

22 When the time of their purification according to the Law of Moses had been completed, Joseph and Mary took him to Jerusalem to present him to the Lord

23 (as it is written in the Law of the Lord, "Every firstborn male is to be consecrated to the Lord")

24 and to offer a sacrifice in keeping with what is said in the Law of the Lord: "a pair of doves or two young pigeons."

33 The child's father and mother marveled at what was said about him.

34 Then Simeon blessed them and said to Mary, his mother: "This child is destined to cause the falling and rising of many in Israel, and to be a sign that will be spoken against,

35 so that the thoughts of many hearts will be revealed. And a sword will pierce your own soul too."

Reference to Proverbs 31

Verse 20: "She opens her arms to the poor
and extends her hands to the needy."

Related Bible References

At the time of the Passover, God struck down the firstborn of the Egyptians, the last straw that finally convinced Pharaoh to let the Israelites leave. At the same time, in Exodus 13:1-2, he requests that all firstborn males among the Israelites be consecrated to him. The animals were literally sacrificed, and the sons were consecrated in a temple ceremony, as Jesus is here.

Additionally, after childbirth, a mother of any child, boy or girl, is instructed in Leviticus 12:1-8 to sacrifice a lamb and a pigeon or dove, or if she is poor, two doves or pigeons. Mary does not feel the need to go into debt or spend money she and Joseph cannot prudently spare to pay for a lamb and make a better show of this event. She knows God in his mercy has made provision for the poor in his law with the intention of helping people like herself. Later, when she has the means, she will assist those in need by following Jesus on his travels and caring for him and his friends.

Questions Regarding This Incident in Mary's Life

1. Did even Mary and Joseph, the most perfect of parents, need the support of the faith community (the "village") to raise their child?
2. Did the presentation ceremony help them acknowledge and fulfill this need?

Reflection

At the time of the Annunciation, Mary accepted Jesus for herself (Lk 1:38). She then joyfully shared him with her cousin Elizabeth in the Visitation (Lk 1:46-55). At the Nativity, she shared Jesus with Joseph, the shepherds, and the wise men (Lk 2:8-20 and Mt 2:1-12). No one knows whether or not she talked about her son's divine nature with the Egyptians while she lived among them (Mt 2:13-15, Scene 2). She may have, since the Egyptians were highly spiritual in their own way and might have been at least mildly interested and receptive. Now, in this scene, Mary shares Jesus with the people of God, the other believers in him.

Joseph and Mary take the time to listen to Simeon and Anna as they speak with them at some length in the temple. They are not in a hurry to "get on with their lives," or anxious because the ceremony is taking longer than would normally be expected. Instead, they see the arrival of these prophets as the occasion of grace that it is. We, too, can take time to listen to others who may be saying something God wants us to hear, either in person or by reading their words in the good spiritual books of our own time and of times past.

While we don't formally consecrate our firstborn children to God as the Israelites did, we do give them to God in the sacrament of baptism. Ideally, when we have a child baptized, we don't do it with the intention of limiting the ways the Holy Spirit can express God's will through that child. But nonetheless, many parents seem horrified at the thought of their son becoming a priest or their daughter becoming a nun. Perhaps one reason our church has a shortage of priests and sisters is that so many of us find it so hard to give our children to God unconditionally, as Joseph and Mary did with Jesus.

Mary may have known exactly what Simeon meant when he said that a sword would pierce her soul because of her son. After all, it would be the leaders of this same temple where they were standing who would ultimately condemn Jesus to death. (Simeon and Anna would by then be long gone and unable to influence the chief priests' decision, and in any case it is likely that no one in power would have listened to them.) At that time, Mary would not be able to do what she could do now: bundle Jesus up and carry him back to the peace, security, and safety of Nazareth.

Questions Relating the Story to Our Lives and Times

1. How can we make prescribed religious rituals into meaningful experiences that integrate us and our families into the community of believers?

2. How can we celebrate spiritual milestones such as first communion and confirmation so that the child has no doubt of the importance of these sacraments?

3. How can we find the time to listen to people who may be speaking to us with God's voice, as Simeon and Anna prophesied to Joseph and Mary?

Scene 4

Mary Follows Jesus on His Divine Mission (Luke 8:19–21)

19 Now Jesus' mother and brothers came to see him, but they were not able to get near him because of the crowd.
20 Someone told him, "Your mother and brothers are standing outside, wanting to see you."
21 He replied, "My mother and brothers are those who hear God's word and put it into practice."

Reference to Proverbs 31

Verse 27: "She watches over the affairs of her household, and does not eat the bread of idleness."

Related Bible References

Both the Old and New Testaments make it clear that those who carry out God's will, not simply those born into a privileged state of chosenness, will be the ones he accepts. In the Old Testament, God makes his covenant with his people, but as in any sacrament the benefit is dependent not only on God, who is unchanging and perfect, but on the disposition of the believer who meets him in the sacrament.

When Jesus heals the centurion's servant (Mt 8:5-13), he shows that God's mercy is not dependent on one's race or national origin. He emphasizes this point in verse 11, where he tells the crowd with him at Capernaum, "Many will come from the east and the west, and will take their places at the feast with Abraham, Isaac, and Jacob in the kingdom of heaven." In contrast, in Matthew 23:1-39 he denounces the hypocritical scribes and Pharisees, who make life difficult for the less elite believers (v. 4) but then bend the law to mean something it never intended when it suits their interests (vv. 16-22).

Jesus is not insulting his family here. He is just pointing out that it is their faith put into practice that will save them, not their special relationship to him on Earth.

Questions Regarding This Incident in Mary's Life

1. Do you think Mary was offended when she heard what her son's response was to her request to see him?
2. How did Jesus use this incident as a teaching tool?

Reflection

Mary was accustomed to travel, having visited Elizabeth while pregnant, then fleeing into Egypt with a newborn. Now she is on the road again, following her son on his travels and no doubt caring for him in material ways. Despite the culture in which she lived, she displays great independence and resourcefulness merely by keeping up with Jesus, who is himself always on the move. Mary knows from the Cana incident that Jesus is on his own, and she no longer bears any responsibility for him, but she follows because, like the apostles, she wants to be with him all the time.

Jesus' use of what we now call "inclusive language" is interesting here. We often hear the term "brothers in Christ," but how often do we think of what it means to be a *mother* to Jesus? Yet in a world teeming with people who are wretchedly poor, driven from their homes by war or economic desperation, abandoned because of mental illness or addictions, or otherwise in desperate need of care, perhaps what is needed most is people who will act as kind and nurturing mothers to those who have no one to care for them. And if we try to think of someone who did this, who comes to mind but the late *Mother* Teresa?

A recent book that questions the importance of parents in the upbringing of children asserts that the child's peer group has a far greater influence than the mother or father on the personal qualities, success, or failure of a child. While crediting or blaming the parents alone for the later behavior of their children is clearly extreme, and also unbiblical, the importance Jesus gave to his mother in his life on Earth and to the role of mother in this passage suggests that mothers are very important in God's eyes, if not in those of some writers.

If we think about what a good mother does, we see there are many ways we can be a mother to Jesus. We can give him "quality time" but also "quantity time"; avoid favoring material things above our relationship with him; never be too busy to listen; praise much and criticize little; always stand by him, even when we don't understand what he is doing; treat him with compassion and kindness when others hurt him; and finally, give him the best we have to offer in accord with our means and our talents.

Questions Relating the Story to Our Lives and Times

1. In what ways can each of us act as a mother to Jesus on an ordinary day?
2. How can we give Jesus time from our lives every day, as a mother would do for her child?
3. How can we maintain our faith and hope in God when it seems as though our prayers are not "getting through"? How can we be patient when what we are asking is apparently far more urgent to us than it is to God? Can you recall a time you waited a long period for a prayer to be answered, and when it finally was, the result far exceeded your expectations?

Scene 5

Mary Shares with Jesus in His Darkest Hour (John 19:25–27)

25 Near the cross of Jesus stood his mother, his mother's sister, Mary the wife of Clopas, and Mary Magdalene.
26 When Jesus saw his mother there, and the disciple whom he loved standing nearby, he said to his mother, "Dear woman, here is your son,"
27 and to the disciple, "Here is your mother." From that time on, this disciple took her into his home.

Reference to Proverbs 31

Verse 15: "She gets up while it is still dark;
　　　　　she provides food for her family and portions
　　　　　　for her servant girls."

Related Bible References

Toward its end, the Gospel of John begins referring to John as "the disciple whom Jesus loved." Here, after the resurrection, when John recognizes Jesus on the beach (Jn 21:7), and at the very end, when Jesus gives his final instructions to Peter and John (Jn 21:20), this disciple is identified as the one whom Jesus loved in some special way.

The first reference to John as the one whom Jesus loved is at the Last Supper, in John 13:23-25. John rests on Jesus' breast, near his heart, at this critical time. Perhaps John already knew, before Jesus made it clear in the scene that took place as he was dying, that although Peter had the keys to the kingdom (Mt 16:19), John had been given the keys to his heart. No wonder references to the love of God permeate his Gospel more than any of the others!

Questions Regarding This Incident in Mary's Life

1. Why did Jesus choose John to take Mary into his home after his return to the Father?

2. Why did Mary need to live with someone else, rather than just live alone?

Reflection

Jesus knew that Mary would soon join him in heaven, but nonetheless set her mind at ease regarding the duration of her time on Earth by giving her specific instructions as to where she was to go after his departure. Just as in Scene 1, where he entrusts her to the care of Joseph, God shows he intends to protect Mary at all times. He also gives John an incomparable privilege by in effect saying that John would take Jesus' place in Jesus' earthly family after he was no longer with them.

After his resurrection, Jesus does not ascend to the Father without giving priceless gifts to all who had followed and stood by him, even if they had failed and stumbled from time to time just as we all do. Of course, the greatest gift to all the disciples was the promise of the Paraclete, fulfilled shortly after his return to heaven (see Scene 6). Jesus also gave the gift of forgiveness to Peter, who had denied him (Jn 21:15-19). John's gift was the continuing presence of Mary, Jesus' perfect mother, in his life.

We, too, experience these gifts as people of the resurrection. The Holy Spirit does speak to our hearts when we let prayer become central in our lives. When we confess our sins, we have Jesus' assurance that he has given his church the power to forgive sin in his name. And when we ask Mary to intercede for us, we know that, despite our shortcomings, Jesus' mother can present our requests in such a pleasing way that her divine son will be hard put to refuse what we ask.

Mary was the first disciple to meditate on the passion and death of Jesus. We can grow spiritually from this devotion, too. How can we doubt the love of Jesus or be afraid of God if we have been contemplating what he was willing to suffer for us? We can then pray with great confidence, our whole heart filled with the faith, hope, and love that Saint Paul tells us are the only things that last (1 Cor 13:13).

Mary is the mother of all of us, Catholic or not, Christian or not. The other saints are our brothers and sisters in Christ, but Mary is the only saint we call our mother. Some of the prayers of the saints to Mary may seem exaggerated and overdone in their expressions of devotion to her. However, because of her special place as our mother, she is properly honored with a unique devotion. Her universal motherhood may one day draw people of all races and religions together, and heal our centuries-old divisions.

Questions Relating the Story to Our Lives and Times

1. How can we discern the needs of our own parents as they age? How can we fulfill these needs without intruding on their privacy or hurting their feelings?

2. What do parents need and want most from their adult children?

3. In what ways do parents and children remain responsible for, and accountable to, each other for their entire lifetimes? In what ways are they required to let go?

Scene 6

Mary Prays with the Apostles for the Coming of the Paraclete (Acts of the Apostles 1:12-14)

12 Then they returned to Jerusalem from the hill called the Mount of Olives, a Sabbath day's walk from the city.
13 When they arrived, they went upstairs to the room where they were staying. Those present were Peter, John, James and Andrew; Philip and Thomas, Bartholomew and Matthew; James son of Alphaeus and Simon the Zealot, and Judas son of James.
14 They all joined together constantly in prayer, along with the women and Mary the mother of Jesus, and with his brothers.

Reference to Proverbs 31

Verse 26: "She speaks with wisdom,
and faithful instruction is on her tongue."

Related Bible References

When Jesus left them by ascending into heaven, the disciples must have felt like the exiled Jews of the Old Testament. He had promised to send them the Holy Spirit, but they probably didn't know what this meant, even though the prophets had predicted this. For example, in Ezekiel 36:24-27, God promises to bring the people back to the Promised Land, purify them (v. 25), put a new heart in them (v. 26), and then put his Spirit in them (v. 27).

In the book of Joel, we find a fuller explanation of what this will mean. In Joel 2:28-32, God promises that when his Spirit is poured forth on his people, their sons and daughters will prophesy (v. 28), and even their servants, both men and women, will receive the gift of the Spirit (v. 29). This prophecy is fulfilled by the coming of the Holy Spirit at Pentecost (Acts 2:1-21), as Peter points out to the crowd in verses 17-21, quoting these verses.

Questions Regarding This Incident in Mary's Life

1. Why did the believers pray before beginning to preach about Jesus' resurrection?

2. How did they know the Holy Spirit would come to them?

Reflection

In this passage, we see evidence already that the emerging church will be led primarily by the disciples who had followed

Jesus throughout the years of his ministry. Though many women had also followed him all that time and were present in the "upper room" scene described here, only one is mentioned by name: Mary, his mother, who already appears to have a place of honor among the believers.

We know from Mary's Magnificat (see Luke 1:46-55, discussed in Words 3 and 4) that her vision included future generations. Nonetheless, the view that prevailed in the early church was that Jesus would return soon, in the lifetime of many of the converts. We don't know whether or not Mary discussed or debated this issue with any of the apostles or other leaders, but if she did they apparently didn't listen.

There was no question that Mary was supposed to be with the disciples, since John was there, and as we saw in Scene 5, Mary had been entrusted to his care by Jesus himself. She may have followed John on his travels, or perhaps she was taken into heaven before any of the apostles began their missionary journeys. The latter seems likely, since she is not mentioned anywhere else in the Book of Acts.

One lesson we can learn from this scene is that prayer must precede action, even in the case of people with strong faith that is based on eyewitness evidence. It is not enough to be fully convinced for oneself, as the disciples already were. If we don't put prayer first, whatever we try to do instead will not bear the fruit that it should have. We can remember the case of the post-exile Israelites, who built beautiful homes for themselves while neglecting the house of God (Hg 1:4). Through the prophet Haggai, God points out that because of this, the Israelites' efforts yield far less than would normally be expected (Hg 1:5-6, 9-11). In contrast, the example of the believers at

Pentecost shows the power of prayer and of giving everything over to God's will.

In our time, there is a popular saying, "You can only change yourself," and before the Paraclete came it may have seemed to the disciples that this was the case. But when the Holy Spirit came to them, it told them the opposite—that with the help of power from heaven, they could change the whole world! Perhaps they heard in this call an echo of the Spirit-inspired prophecy of Simeon, who told Mary and Joseph that Jesus would change the world (Lk 2:28-35). And perhaps also, if we pray and listen first, we can follow the example of these first disciples and rebuild our church and our nation.

Questions Relating the Story to Our Lives and Times

1. What is the role of consecrated women, and women in the church in general, in our time? How has this changed from former times?

2. How can these women use the gifts of the Spirit for the benefit of the entire Christian community?

3. How can we discover what gifts the Holy Spirit has given to us, and how God wants us to use them?

Scene 7

Mary Takes Her Place in Heaven (Revelation 12:1-6)

1   A great and wondrous sign appeared in heaven: a woman clothed with the sun, with the moon under her feet and a crown of twelve stars on her head.
2   She was pregnant and cried out in pain as she was about to give birth.
3   Then another sign appeared in heaven: an enormous red dragon with seven heads and ten horns and seven crowns on his heads.
4   His tail swept a third of the stars out of the sky and flung them to the earth. The dragon stood in front of the woman who was about to give birth, so that he might devour her child the moment it was born.
5   She gave birth to a son, a male child, who will rule all the nations with an iron scepter. And her child was snatched up to God and to his throne.
6   The woman fled into the desert to a place prepared for her by God, where she might be taken care of for 1,260 days.

Reference to Proverbs 31

Verse 25: "She is clothed with strength and dignity;
	she can laugh at the days to come."

Related Bible References

Full interpretation of the symbolism used in the Book of Revelation is beyond the scope of this book. Even after two thousand years, much of its meaning remains obscure and is debated by theologians of all faiths, including our own. But the symbol here of the queen of heaven giving birth to a child whom Satan wants to destroy but whom God preserves so that he can some day rule the nations seems unmistakable.

In her glorious appearance here, the woman resembles the royal bride of Psalm 45, who takes her place at God's right hand arrayed in the gold of Ophir (v. 9). Like this royal bride, Mary put all else behind her to serve God from the day she first received word from the angel that she had been specially chosen by him. Like that bride, she and her companions are "led in with joy and gladness; they enter the palace of the king" (Ps 45:15). And in this vision, that is where John sees her.

Questions Regarding This Incident in Mary's Life

1. How do we know that the woman in Revelation 12 is Mary?

2. How does Mary's example and destiny compare with that of Eve? Does Mary, too, lead humanity in a new direction?

Reflection

Images of power and beauty are seldom associated with pregnancy in our culture, or in many others either. Yet this powerful image of Mary in heaven, crowned in the beauty of heaven as its queen, giving birth to the son of God himself, certainly demolishes many stereotypes about both women and childbearing.

Even under the stress of childbirth, Mary does not appear to be afraid of the dragon that has come to devour her child. She trusts in God and does what he asks of her, which in this case is naturally quite clear. God snatches the child up to himself and doesn't forget about her, either, when her work is complete. He ensures that she will be safe despite war and destruction on every side. This can serve as reassurance to us, too, that if we are faithful to our calling, we also need not fear anything that may happen in the future, in this world or the next!

Mary is sometimes compared to the moon, as Jesus is compared to the sun (Mal 4:2). This makes sense, since by her words and actions she reflects the light of God, just as the moon reflects the light of the sun down onto the Earth at night. When our hearts seem to be in darkness, and God seems far away, we can think of Mary's words and example and recognize the light of God shining in them. And just as the moon's light promises that the sun is still shining and will rise at its proper time, Mary taking her place in heaven reminds us that Jesus will return at the appointed time, just as he promised.

Mary's place in heaven encourages us to continue on our spiritual walk in Christ, for Mary is just like us in most ways. She was created by God to glorify him; she was also born and then lived her life on the same Earth that we now inhabit. In heaven, she is a sign of our future union with God. Her example shows our importance in God's plans, a sign to us that by God's grace, the finite can affect the Infinite.

At the time of his ascension, Jesus promised his apostles he would not leave them orphans. He kept that promise by sending them the Holy Spirit at Pentecost and by giving them his mother for all time. Both are still with us—and these are signs that we will never be orphans! We are all God's beloved children, with Jesus as our brother and Mary as our mother.

Questions Relating the Story to Our Lives and Times

1. In this story, God provides a place for Mary out in the desert, apart from the rest of the world. For what purposes do we sometimes seclude ourselves from the distractions of the world?

2. Should Christian women think of themselves first as daughters of Eve, or as daughters of Mary? What qualities that we see in ourselves remind us of one or the other of these foremothers?

3. How will this affect our attitudes toward ourselves and our calling in God?

Conclusion

We have now reached the end of these reflections. Anyone who wishes to learn more about Mary will find an abundance of books to help them, from this publisher's catalog and from many others. Learning about Mary is a lifelong process, as is true of all aspects of our faith. The Bible's treasures are inexhaustible; how many we find depends only on how much time and effort we are willing to spend digging for them.

The words of Mary are enhanced by the dramatic power of the events of her life. Her entire life expresses the central mystery of our faith, that of God's presence among us. In her youth, Mary prepared her heart to do God's will, so that her acceptance of the angel's invitation flowed naturally and joyfully. She then followed her divine son through all his travels and finally to Calvary. Finally, she was present at the founding of the church after Jesus' ascension. All of us, too, share in these mysteries as we meditate on them and allow them to shape our hearts and direct our actions.

For me, meditating on the life of Mary has always been life enhancing and empowering. Everything Mary does comes from her free gift of herself to her God, which in turn sets her free from all worldly constraints and limitations. Everything she says to us, and everything she does in these additional scenes, has a power beyond mere human words and actions, because Mary had committed herself fully to God. By this means, even in rather primitive times, one woman could—and did—change history forever.

Like the mother in Proverbs 31, Mary is wise and well-spoken, a mother on whom we can always rely for gracious help, good counsel, and a powerful example to follow. Unlike our very first mother Eve, Mary obeyed God and did not rebel at what he asked of her. She carried it out, so that in her we might all find blessing in the fulfillment of God's promises through the prophets. We can join our voices with those of the children of the mother in Proverbs 31, knowing that it is right for us to "Arise and call her blessed" (Prv 31:28). Toward this end, I would like to conclude with the last two verses of Proverbs 31:

30 Charm is deceptive, and beauty is fleeting;
but a woman who fears the Lord is to be praised.
31 Give her the reward she has earned,
and let her works bring her praise at the city gate.